ENGLISH
IN
THE UNIVERSITIES

CAMBRIDGE
UNIVERSITY PRESS

University Printing House, Cambridge CB2 8BS, United Kingdom

Published in the United States of America by Cambridge University Press, New York

Cambridge University Press is part of the University of Cambridge.

It furthers the University's mission by disseminating knowledge in the pursuit of education, learning and research at the highest international levels of excellence.

www.cambridge.org
Information on this title: www.cambridge.org/9781107634466

First published 1945
Re-issued 2014

A catalogue record for this publication is available from the British Library

ISBN 978-1-107-63446-6 Paperback

ENGLISH

IN

THE UNIVERSITIES

AN INAUGURAL LECTURE

BY

JAMES SUTHERLAND

Professor of English at Queen Mary College
University of London

CAMBRIDGE

At the University Press

1945

An Inaugural Lecture to the Chair of English Language and Literature in the University of London (Queen Mary College), delivered in the Arts Lecture Theatre, Mill Lane, in the fifth year of the College's evacuation to Cambridge. The Provost of King's College presided.

ENGLISH IN THE UNIVERSITIES

THE subject of 'English in the Universities' seemed to me to be a natural choice for an inaugural lecture; it raises interesting and important issues, and it is a matter on which I felt that I had a good deal to say. I have not changed my mind about the interest and importance of the subject; but the more I have considered it, the more I have come to realise that what I had thought of as an interesting field for discussion has been developing in recent years into something much more like a battleground. Anyone who ventures upon this ground is almost bound to find himself taking sides, whether he wants to or not; and even if I manage to avoid doing that, the chances are that my little jeep, out on nothing more than a harmless reconnaissance, will be blown to pieces by one side or the other. But I wish to make it clear at the outset that what I have to say about English in the universities is offered as a purely personal statement; and I must ask for a certain amount of indulgence if at times it comes nearer to being a confession of faith than an inaugural lecture.

Before I say anything about what I think we ought to teach our students, I want to say something about those students themselves. The men and women I should like to see studying English in my own department are, as Wordsworth put it, 'the young of both sexes [to whom] poetry is, like love, a passion'; who are so much moved, in fact, when they read aloud a piece of great literature that they can hardly trust themselves to go on. That, at any rate, would be my first test. I would put into the hands of the prospective student, say, Florizel's speech to Perdita in *The Winter's Tale*—the speech that begins:

> What you do
> Still betters what is done...

and continues with:

> when you do dance, I wish you
> A wave o' the sea, that you might ever do
> Nothing but that; move still, still so,
> And own no other function.

If I found my candidate showing signs of trouble half-way through, I would say to him: 'You'll do. There's probably a lot you don't know yet, and if you want to be a good English scholar there is scarcely any kind of knowledge that won't be useful to you. But even if you know almost nothing *now*, you are the sort of person I want to teach, because I can see that poetry is more to you than a series of statements. You have a feeling for words; you are alive to those rhythms and harmonies upon which so much of the full enjoyment of literature will always depend.'

If anyone should think that I am being precious or affected in suggesting that this sort of immediate response is the first thing needed, I would ask him to consider if it is not rather odd that anyone should be encouraged to study—and, still more, to pass judgments upon—one of the great literatures of the world, if it is to mean little more to him than a series of facts or statements. A full and adequate response to the work of a great writer will depend on many things; but probably the most essential is the ability to respond to words and rhythm, to the cadence of English speech, English prose, English verse, to the sound-value of the words themselves and in combination, and to the complete fusion of words and meaning. How many people have this equipment? If we are to judge by the way some scholars write, a sensitiveness to the values of words is often wanting in those who give their lives to literary studies. We ought to be shocked at this. What shocks me is how little we *are* shocked. When I meet with critics who invite me to find fault with Milton or Shelley in prose that sets my teeth on edge, or who call for delicacy of perception in the harsh voice of a Holofernes, I am lost in wonder. I wonder, but I also suspect.

So I put this first in my demands of the student of English: that he should be sensitive to the medium of prose and of poetry, that he should be able to respond to the mere sound of great literature. As a teacher I may be able to widen and deepen and sharpen that response, but I know that I can do very little if that organic sensibility is not there in the first place. And heaven forbid that I should try—that I should encourage anyone to go through the motions of response, or lead him to suppose that anything can take its place. A teacher of painting would give short shrift to an art student who turned out to be colour-blind, and a teacher of music would not wish to persevere with a pupil who was tone-deaf. And if these unpromising pupils, abandoning the *practice*, were to take to the criticism of art or music, we should, if we knew the facts, be rightly indignant. Yet when we find a student of English literature who shows by his way of reading half a dozen lines of Shakespeare that he has little sense of either the rhythm of speech or the rhythm of blank verse, and still less of the delicate adjustment of the one to the other, we rarely think of suggesting to him that he might do better to study History or Economics, or some other subject in which the only function of words is to be clear and precise.

I have said, uncompromisingly, what I want. But what I want is not always what I shall get. Perhaps half of my pupils will have the kind of sensibility that I should like to see in all of them. What is to be done with the rest? Why are they there at all? Some of them, as all teachers of English know, are there because English is commonly supposed to be an easy subject, even in London, where we still include papers in Old and Middle English and in the History of the Language. But I am convinced that the majority of them are reading English because they like it, and prefer it to any other subject. It is true, they may feel more at home with the drama and the novel than with Blake and Shelley; but they enjoy what they read, and can with good teaching be brought to enjoy it still more. Nor is there any reason to suppose that intellectually they will not be the equals of the others, and some of them will probably obtain a first class. I shall be told that I have already condemned them as students of English. No; I have only said that they are not to me the ideal students. Some of them may develop into very useful people indeed—literary historians, philologists, bibliographers, and so on; and others will pass into the schools and become good teachers, though not, I think, the very best sort of teachers.

My analogy with the student of art or music, though not altogether beside the point, was, in fact, defective. I do not wish to retract anything I have already said; but it must be obvious that a genuine enjoyment of literature is possible even if the reader is not particularly sensitive to the values of words and the subtleties of rhythm. With literature the enjoyment is much more an intellectual matter than it is with painting, and it is much more complex. A good deal of *Julius Caesar* or *Tom Jones* would be left even in an inferior translation: there would still be the interest of plot and characters and manners and thought. My second type of student would be perfectly happy with all of those, and they are all proper interests of the student of literature.

Pope's friend Allen, Lord Bathurst, used to refer to Matthew Prior as his 'verse-man', and to Erasmus Lewis as his 'prose-man'. That, roughly, brings out the distinction I have been trying to make between the two types of student we have to teach. I love the verse-men, but I respect the prose-men. And there is plenty of good work

9

for the prose-men to do in the fields of literary history, literary theory, the history of ideas, and in literary and linguistic research of all kinds. It is they who will tell us what sort of education Shakespeare had, the sort of stage he wrote for, how his plays were acted, how they came to be printed, and many other useful and even indispensable facts. I am afraid they will also write many erudite articles, such as 'John Smith's "Brief Description of the Tribe of Monkeys" as a possible source for "The Voyage to the Houyhnhnms"', or 'Shelley's Debt to Phineas Fletcher for the Fifteenth Stanza of his "Adonais"': they will deal freely in tendencies and influences and parallel passages and literary reputations; they will be notable collectors of data and evidence. Let us take them at their best, however, and we shall have much cause to be grateful to them. And I, for one, never forget that I may have some future historian of the Theatre or the Novel or the Newspaper sitting in my Honours class,

> The baby figure of the giant mass
> Of things to come at large.

Good luck to him; and all honour to him if in the course of years he becomes a Sir Edmund Chambers, or even something half as good. I would only ask of him that, like Wordsworth's poet, he would shine quietly in his place, and be content.

I have distinguished, then, between two types of student which past experience has taught me to expect. No doubt I have made the distinction too absolute: many students will be somewhere betwixt and between. In any case, it would be a mistake, I believe, to attempt to differentiate between them in actual teaching, or at any rate to differentiate much. For one thing it often takes me a considerable time to discover what sort of student I have to deal with, and I have made enough mistakes in the past to realise that my first impressions may be wrong. For another thing, I want my first type of student—the versemen—to acquire as much literary and historical knowledge as may reasonably be expected of them in two or three years. They must, of course, continue to respond freely and naturally to what they read, but that is not enough. They should be steadily acquiring literary experience. They cannot forever be looking into Chapman's Homer for the first time. If, as lovers of literature, they are ever to pass beyond the stage of what Wordsworth called 'aching joys' and 'dizzy raptures', they will have to learn to look on literature 'not as in the hour of thoughtless youth'. In short, they will have to get knowledge. I want to see the Schools of English in our universities producing not just lively persons able to talk briskly and brightly about English literature—not just critics, but scholar-critics.

Unquestionably, there is a great deal of English literature (more particularly in the last hundred and fifty years) that requires little comment or explanation, but there is also much that is not fully and immediately intelligible to the twentieth-century reader. There is also a good deal, of course, that may *seem* to yield up its meaning at first sight, but contains further layers of reference that are not immediately apparent. Not to labour this point, I would say that our habits and customs are continually changing, our environment, our whole way of thought, our language (both written and spoken), our education (both in form and content). They all change, and with them goes a change in 'what every schoolboy knows'. With all those changes it becomes a more and more difficult and delicate business to read the great literature of the past as it ought to be read.

I have not forgotten that there are such people as editors, who make it their business to elucidate hard passages and to excavate buried allusions, and I would be the last person to wish to derogate from their importance. Nobody really likes editors, and nobody really appreciates them except other editors. They shall have no hard words from me. But the work they do, however necessary, is almost inevitably distracting to the reader, if only because it reminds him of his ignorance. There is something irritating about even the best footnote. 'Ah', it seems to say, 'I thought that would puzzle you: well, I'll tell you what it means.' Or, worse still: 'Ah, you thought you understood that passage, didn't you? Well, as a matter of fact you didn't. Look, I will explain it to you.' If it is a choice between light and darkness, I suppose we should all prefer the farthing candle of the editor to complete ignorance. But what is needed, of course, is the flash of illumination *as we actually read*.

There are three stages in the progress from darkness to

light. The first is complete and utter ignorance—the words make no sense at all. In the second stage the difficulty is explained by the editor or the teacher. In this way some of Chaucer's jokes were explained to me when I was a schoolboy. I was told that Chichevache was a fabulous monster who lived on patient wives. I accepted the information and smiled as in duty bound. The only joke which I discovered for myself was the one about the Prioress, who spoke French

> ......ful faire and fetisly,
> After the school of Stratford atte Bowe.

But it was then pointed out to me that modern scholars had satisfactorily shown that this was not a joke at all, but a perfectly serious statement, and I withdrew my laughter accordingly. In this second stage, at any rate, the student has the satisfaction of not being left in a completely puzzled state of mind. Whether he is interested in what he has learnt or not, he has at least got an explanation. That is something. But I suggest that it is not nearly enough.

My third stage is much further on, and it is one which it would be unfair to expect the undergraduate to reach in two or three years. It is nothing less than being able to read the literature of the past with the immediate awareness of the present—to read the *Epistle to Dr. Arbuthnot* as Arbuthnot read it, or to read *Julius Caesar* as Ben Jonson may have read it in the First Folio. The ideal, I will readily admit, is not completely attainable, and we can never tell how far we fall short of it. In one sense, too, it is not even desirable; or, at any rate, that is not the only way we ought to read. We must also read from our own modern standpoint. But though I can agree that the literary criticism of every generation is necessarily concerned to a large extent with re-assessing the great works of the past, and saying how they look to us, and what value they have for us to-day, I ask more of the literary critic than that. He must also get me out of my own time; he must help me to understand the mind of past ages.

The scholar-critic, in fact, has two very different tasks to perform. He must, in the first place, be able to bring out what is permanent in the literature of the past. What is permanent—whether it turns up in Plato's Dialogues, or in Chaucer, or in More's *Utopia*—is the sort of thing that makes people exclaim, 'How modern!' But this permanent appeal may sometimes be hidden, or partly concealed, by much that is only temporary. When the work in question was contemporary, no one noticed these transitory elements in it, simply because they formed part of the general thought or stylistic convention of the age. When we happen still to like these transitory features in the work of an earlier day, we make remarks like 'How quaint!' When we do not like them, we say things like 'How artificial!' or 'How tedious!'

So the second great task for the scholar-critic is to re-create for us the milieu into which a work of art was born; not so that he may blur the distinction between the permanent and the transitory, but so that he may widen the possibilities of our enjoyment. No doubt the scholar is always in danger of valuing the old and obscure merely because they are so; but ideally he is the reader whose enjoyment is not hindered and interrupted by the old and obscure since he is so entirely familiar with them. He has become a naturalised citizen of the past, or, more probably, of his own favourite century; he has for the time being consciously adopted the unconscious assumptions of past generations; he has learnt their speech and their manners and even their prejudices. No one is more misleading than the critic who attempts, without sufficient knowledge, to translate the past into terms of the present. With enough intelligence and imagination to perceive that Chaucer and Spenser are not just literary antiques, he may nevertheless, in his anxiety to make them available to the twentieth century, pass over the very real differences in thought and feeling that separate us from those poets, and exaggerate or falsify or 'modernise' the resemblances. There is no short cut here. If I am to understand, say, John Bunyan, I must become familiar with his intellectual and social and religious background. I could see for myself that he was a godly sort of man, but I should want to know much more about the peculiar form his godliness took. I should want to *account* for Bunyan, partly to satisfy my natural curiosity, but mainly to enable me to enjoy his work more fully; for if I am puzzled I am probably hostile, and if I am hostile my response is deadened.

Now, if this sort of work is not to be done in our

universities, where is it to be done? We can all be trusted to read Shakespeare from the point of view of the twentieth century; the difficulty is to read him in his own time. I know the danger here—the danger that we may try to turn our students into good Elizabethans, and succeed to such an extent that they can hardly see Shakespeare at all for their knowledge of stage conditions at the Globe, or their knowledge of seventeenth-century melancholy, or Machiavelli, or Elizabethan rhetoric, and so forth. But the danger is not, in my experience, acute.

I have said that the ideal towards which the student of English literature should strive is that flash of illumination as he reads. But it must have been immediately obvious that this flash of illumination is not, unfortunately, the result of intelligence and awareness and imagination only; it will depend as often as not on the contents of the reader's mind. That is what I meant when I said that there is almost no sort of knowledge that will not be useful to the student of English literature. In that intelligent and original book, *The Handling of Words*, Vernon Lee kept on reminding us that what the writer is doing all the time is playing upon the contents of the reader's mind. 'The Writer's materials', she says, 'are words, and it is by arranging these that he copies, so to speak, his own feelings and ideas. But these words, you must remember, are merely *signals* which call up the various items—visual, audible, tactile, emotional, and of a hundred different other sorts—which have been deposited by chance in the mind of the Reader.... The

Writer is really playing upon the contents of the Reader's mind, as the pianist, although his fingers touch only the keyboard, is really playing on the strings. And the response to the manipulation is due, in both cases, to the quality of what is at first not visible: the Reader's potential images and emotions, the string which can be made to vibrate.'[1] And she goes on to add that the efficacy of any word or class of words must depend upon the particular experience of the individual reader.

The writer, then, is at the mercy of every reader's experience, and that must depend partly upon age and opportunity; we obtain much of this experience simply by going on living, and sharing in the common lot of the human race. But there is another kind that we acquire more deliberately, when we read. For a poet like Milton or Pope, an important part of the experience involved will be our previous reading. Pope often expects his reader not just to recognise a reference to Virgil or Horace, but to recall the whole context. It is from such associations that he obtains most of his overtones. To one sort of reader Pope's poetry will be hard and sharp and clear like an etching; to another sort of reader, aware of those secondary values, it will have the delicate shades and the misty suggestions of a Whistler.

I hope I am alive to the danger of turning the study of English into a matter of classical or historical knowledge. But I cannot forget that there is very little in our literature earlier than, say, 1800 that does not call for some

[1] Vernon Lee, *The Handling of Words*, 1923, pp. 43–4.

such knowledge, and that the reader of Donne and Milton and Pope is likely to need a good deal of it. No doubt examiners in search of questions to set have sometimes concentrated too much on what the authors of the 'Norwood' Report rightly call 'the secondary aspects of the books that are being read'. But that does not relieve the student of the necessity of trying to understand what he is reading. And his success, and therefore his enjoyment, will depend not only upon his bare understanding of the words a writer is using, but also upon his response to their literary associations, and to the literary and historical allusions which the writer may be making. No eighteenth-century critic would have questioned the importance of those for one moment, for a great part of the pleasure he obtained from poetry was derived from them. 'Half or more of the beauties of poetry', William Shenstone once remarked, 'depend on metaphor or allusion, neither of which, by a mind uncultivated, can be applied to their proper counterparts. Their beauty of consequence is like a picture to a blind man. How many of these peculiarities in poetry turn upon a knowledge of philosophy and history: and let me add, these latent beauties give the most delight to such as can unfold them.'[1]

Not very long ago I carried out a simple test to ascertain the contents of the reader's mind. Shortly before I had to lecture to a class of about fifty first-year students, I discovered that I had brought the wrong notes with me.

[1] *The Works in Verse and Prose of William Shenstone, Esq.,...* 1764, vol. II, pp. 9–10.

Instead of going in and trying to keep my wicket up for the best part of an hour, I decided to put the class in to bat. So I jotted down some questions designed to test my students' knowledge of Classical Literature and Mythology, of the Bible, and of Modern Science. I gave them one minute to answer each question, having explained that the briefest of answers would do, and that all I really wanted to know was whether the word meant anything to them at all, and if so, what. Of course it is disconcerting to have a series of unrelated questions shot at you at intervals of one minute, and no doubt my method fell far short of the minimum requirements for a really scientific experiment. Still, I learnt something.

There were twelve questions in the first section: Who, or what, were Apelles, Briareus, Dido, Lethe, Achates, Polyphemus, Proserpina, Menelaus, Triton, Thule, Deucalion, Tantalus? There were ten questions for the Bible: Who were Jephthah, Gideon, Japhet, Abednego, Zacchaeus, Tobit, Jehu, Bathsheba, Deborah, the young man of Nain? Finally, there were ten for Science: What are torque, Oedipus complex, mendelism, cam, vernalisation, agoraphobia, leucocyte, spectroscope, electrode, catalyst? As there was still a little time left, I added: How many Muses were there? Name them.

The results were startling. Of the forty-two candidates who handed in their papers, only two had heard of either Briareus or Deucalion. To the other forty the names apparently meant no more than, say, Khaikobad and Khaikosru in Omar Khayyám. Those two candidates, on a generous marking, scored eight out of twelve in the classical section. The average for *all* the candidates was about three out of twelve. Among the other names that proved most baffling were Thule, Tantalus, Apelles, Menelaus, and Achates. Tantalus was mixed up with Prometheus and Sisyphus, Achates was said to be a Greek god, the father of Aeneas, and a sea battle. Most of the answers were simply a blank. The names that proved most familiar—or, at any rate, that provoked the greatest response—were Dido, Proserpina, Polyphemus, and Lethe. Yet Polyphemus was described as 'a figure in Greek mythology who had many eyes', 'Cyclops whose eye Aeneas put out', 'one of the giants whose eye was poked out by Jason', and 'a Greek philosopher'. Proserpina was said to be 'the daughter of Circe', the 'daughter of the four seasons', 'a Muse', and 'goddess of Spring, who was seen by Croesus, King of the Underworld', and one candidate simply remarked, 'hair full of snakes—beautiful'. For Dido I got 'Trojan princess', 'Muse', 'mother of Aeneas', 'widow of Aeneas', and 'fell in love with Ulysses'; and for Menelaus, 'a Trojan hero, fought against Greeks', 'King of Troy', and 'has something to do with a monster in a labyrinth'. As for the nine Muses, their number ranged from three to fifteen, and no one could name more than four. Of the several spurious Muses which the occasion brought forth, I note in passing: Thesmorphia, muse of dancing.

Among the ten names from the Bible the best known were Japhet, Abednego, Zacchaeus, and, perhaps surprisingly, the young man of Nain. But there was a good deal of guessing. 'One of the minor prophets' proved to be a useful phrase; it was employed to describe half a dozen different people in my list. Jephthah was the father-in-law of Moses, Jehu was 'either the person through whose head a nail was driven or the person who did it', Deborah was 'Samson's Philistine wife', and so on. On the whole the general average for the Bible was about the same as that for the Classical questions; but as it is impossible to tell whether the questions were relatively harder or easier there is not much basis for a comparison.

Of the answers to the questions in Science I will only say that though they were not in general well done, they were often done better than I could have done them myself in similar circumstances. But they were not so well done as to suggest that scientific knowledge is replacing a rapidly disappearing knowledge of the Bible and the Classics.

I have said that the results of this test were startling. They were startling because so much of the great literature of our country, from the time of Chaucer to the close of the nineteenth century, requires for its full understanding and enjoyment a knowledge which the twentieth-century student no longer seems to command to anything like an adequate extent. The contemporaries of Milton at Cambridge, or Swift at Trinity College, Dublin, or Arnold at Oxford would have answered the Classical and Biblical questions far better than their successors in the twentieth century. Indeed, to ask such questions at all of the young Milton or the young Addison, or even the young Lord Byron, would have been almost an insult.

I will cite one short passage of prose as evidence of the change which has come over English education. In 1790 Edmund Burke published his *Reflections on the Revolution in France*. In the passage that follows he is driving home one of his favourite points: that the state is an organism of slow growth, and that in consequence it should exact from us a reverence that will make us abhor all sudden innovations. 'By this wise prejudice,' he argues,

we are taught to look with horror on those children of their country, who are prompt rashly to hack that aged parent to pieces, and put him into the kettle of magicians, in hopes by their poisonous weeds, and wild incantations, they may regenerate the paternal constitution, and renovate their father's life.[1]

It would be foolish to suppose that all of Burke's readers in the year 1790 took this passage in their stride. Seven thousand copies of his pamphlet are said to have been sold within a week, and almost 20,000 in the first year of its publication. But no doubt there were many of Burke's readers to whom this reference to Medea and the daughters of Pelias meant nothing, or at best something that awakened only vague associations. Yet many, perhaps the majority of them, must have understood his allusion. The story of how the daughters of Pelias cut up their old father and boiled him in a cauldron in the belief that Medea would renew his youth as she had renewed that of old Aeson is

[1] 'World's Classics' ed., p. 105.

to be found in Ovid's *Metamorphoses*, Book VII, a work of which any boy who had been educated in an eighteenth-century grammar school could scarcely be ignorant. About fifty years earlier, Pope had referred to Medea's more successful experiment on her father-in-law:

> ...Thus revive the Wits!
> But murder first, and mince them all to bits;
> As erst Medea (cruel, so to save!)
> A new Edition of old Æson gave.[1]

This then was the sort of knowledge an eighteenth-century poet or prose writer counted upon your having, and owing to the strong classical bias of the eighteenth-century school curriculum he did not count upon it in vain. To-day the response is far less certain. A shift in the emphasis of education has left the twentieth-century reader less well-equipped to respond to those literary associations on which our poets and prose writers were accustomed to play.

Indeed, I am not sure that it is merely a shift in emphasis. I cannot help feeling that we have become so nervous about cramming our children with facts, and so anxious to teach them intelligently, that year after year they know less and less—though no doubt they become more and more intelligent, and better able to deal with facts if only they had the facts to deal with. I am very ready to admit that the teaching of some subjects—Geography is one of them—has improved enormously since I was a schoolboy:

[1] *The Dunciad*, IV, 119 ff. The lines refer to the labours of textual critics and editors.

23

we were asked to commit many things to memory without being given any good reason for doing so. In this way I was made to learn the capes of Great Britain from Cape Wrath to Ardnamurchan Point, and I do not think the knowledge has ever been of the slightest use to me. But nowadays we may be going too far in the opposite direction. Certainly, a great deal of knowledge that would once have been looked upon as essential to any well-educated person is no longer being imparted or acquired.

But to return to the Classics. I have indicated the obvious deficiency there. What is the remedy? In London we have recently experimented in the Honours examination with a new paper called 'The Classical Background of English Literature'. The results so far have been moderately satisfactory. Those who take this paper are expected to have some knowledge of both Greek and Latin, and are tested by passages set for translation. I am not sure how far a course in Greek and Latin Literature and Thought, in which the student was left to read his classical authors in translation, would answer our purpose. It would certainly be better than nothing, and anyone who is too ready to scoff ought to remember John Keats. But I have a suggestion to make. The authors of the 'Norwood' Report deprecate what they call 'a premature external examination of pupils at school in English Literature'. This has naturally caused alarm and despondency among the teachers of English in both schools and universities; for it carries with it the consequence that scholarships will no longer be awarded to candidates in English, and that English studies will necessarily suffer. I do not wish to pronounce here upon the wisdom of this particular recommendation, but I will make my suggestion. It is simply that in allocating State scholarships, a number should be set aside for Classics, to be competed for by boys and girls who wish to read English at the universities. These scholarships would be distinct from those awarded to candidates who intend to continue their classical studies at the university. At one stroke there would be a considerable increase in the study of Latin and Greek in the schools, and English studies at the university stage would benefit from an annual intake of students with a classical background. The Schools of English can hardly be expected to provide that background for their students; but I believe that most of us would be glad if more of our students already had it before they came to us.

If, as some may think, I have over-stressed the advantage of some sort of classical training for the student of English, it is probably because my own reading has lain mostly in the eighteenth century, and I am continually being reminded how large a part classical literature (but Latin more than Greek) played in shaping the thought and the literary style of that century. But I hope that nothing I may have said has given the impression that I regard a knowledge of the classics as the royal road to the study of English literature, or still less as a substitute for it. It is indeed only one of many kinds of knowledge that I should like the student to have, so that he may read the literature of his own country with the fullest possible appreciation of its richness. The study of English literature, it seems to me, calls for an intellectual discipline at least equal to that needed for the study of the classics; it demands great powers of imagination and concentration, and it asks for a very wide range of knowledge. For one thing, English literature is infinitely varied, and it has been going on for a thousand years. I am one of those who think that *Beowulf* is an English poem, and that the study of our literature should begin with it; but if anyone wishes to postpone the birth of English poetry till the time of Chaucer, he has still five and a half centuries of it to reckon with. During those centuries the English spirit may have remained essentially the same; but there have been very great changes in the day-to-day life of Englishmen, in their literary forms, in the things they wrote about, and the kind of pleasure they expected to derive from their reading. And it is not only by Latin and Greek writers that our literature has been influenced, but by those of Italy and France and Spain and Germany, and indeed of almost every European nation at some time and to some degree.

As a bare minimum, therefore, we must require from our students—in addition to their knowledge of English literature—some knowledge of literary theory from the time of Aristotle onwards, since at certain periods critical theory almost determined the forms which the writer was free to use, and the very way in which he was to write. Indeed, literary practice has rarely, until comparatively modern times, been completely divorced from literary theory. We must require some knowledge of European literatures, since our own literature is only a part of the general European culture, and has constantly reflected it. We must require a knowledge of the English language—a language which has all the familiar complications of linguistic study, and which has no convenient 'classical period' which will absolve us from the necessity of studying it at all stages of its development. We must at least encourage our students to familiarise themselves with the social life of different periods, and with the religious and intellectual background. These are, I think, the 'priorities'; but the list of requirements might be extended considerably further.

I shall, however, make only one more demand of the student—that he will always try to treat English literature as no more than a part of the general culture of our race. There is a special responsibility on the Schools of English in our universities to interpret English culture in terms of all the arts—and I am thinking not only of Music, Painting, Architecture and so on, but also of the whole English way of life. Here, as everywhere else, we tend to specialise too much, and to isolate one art, and even one aspect of that art, from another. There is no lack of enthusiasm in this country for the various arts, but it tends to express itself in the activities of sects and coteries. We take up causes (characteristically in England the cause of the neglected or forgotten), we proselytise, we take pleasure in a literary and artistic nonconformity. In

Arnold's words, 'we like and dislike too passionately, too exclusively'. We have little sense in this country of living in a genial atmosphere of culture. This, we are apt to think, is being English, but it was not always so. I dare say I am biased in favour of the eighteenth century, but I wish our own twentieth century—with all its great promise of a new and richer civilisation—could achieve that co-ordination, and even integration, of all the various arts, and that diffusion of the arts through society, that marked the age of Pope and Johnson. What is needed, then, is a more general awareness of English culture in the past, such as is already being fostered by the British Council. Here, as I have suggested, the English Schools in our universities might play a vital part. For if we once got the awareness of what had been, we should be in a fair way to achieving a new integration of the arts with social life, a new twentieth-century English civilisation, to replace that which the nineteenth century wantonly destroyed.

I have said almost nothing about what some may consider to be the chief function of a university School of English: the training of students in literary appreciation and discrimination, the forming of a critical judgment. My own view is that this result (which is of course highly desirable) is not to be best achieved by a frontal attack; and I have therefore placed all the emphasis I can on the understanding and enjoyment of literature rather than on the values to be attached to it. By continually dwelling upon values—particularly with men and women of twenty—we are apt to induce an anxiety complex. 'I rather like this', someone will say, 'but ought I really to like it? What if I am quite wrong, and it is something I oughtn't to like at all? As a matter of fact, now that I come to think of it, I don't believe I do like it.' This sort of result seems to me disastrous. A sound literary judgment is surely produced in much the same way as a sound moral judgment—not by endless instruction and precept and self-examination, but by maintaining a satisfactory condition of general health and by a gradually maturing experience. I do not want my students to think about what they ought to think. And I do not want them to try to think at twenty what they may naturally be thinking at forty.

My own part in all this, as I see it, is to remove obstacles from the path, to break down prejudice and the resistance of ignorance, and, above all, to explain why and how. Looking back, I can see that at eighteen years of age I was in very much that condition described by Keats, neither man nor boy, but in 'that space of life between, in which the soul is in a ferment, the character undecided, the way of life uncertain, the ambition thick-sighted'. I was torn between enthusiasm and prejudice, both, as I now see, the children of ignorance. I liked Shelley; I did not like Pope. But when it was brought home to me that Pope was not trying to do the same thing as Shelley, when I came to see what Pope was after, then the possibilities of enjoyment were enormously increased. It came as a kind of revelation to me that *The Rape of the Lock* was not bad Shelley, but good Pope; for I was now beginning to realise not only what Pope was doing but why he was doing it, and that behind him there lay a culture very different from my own. My experience with Wordsworth was much the same; there, too, prejudice had to be broken down. And if anyone tells me that lectures are no good, I remember my old teacher in Aberdeen, Professor Jack, a Cambridge man, who was to me as a young Scotch student a kind of living Hazlitt. He gave us eyes, he gave us ears. I do not remember that he gave us many judgments, but he constantly helped us to understand and he continually quickened our enjoyment. If I cannot always do that for my own students, I can at least try not to spoil for them the literature on which I lecture. When I walk into a lecture room I sometimes find myself recalling the words with which Keats gave his *Endymion* to the world. 'I hope', he wrote, 'I have not in too late a day touched the beautiful mythology of Greece, and dulled its brightness.' I speak only for myself; but it has always seemed to me, as a person who writes and talks about English literature, that the one thing I must never do is to dull the brightness of Milton or Shelley or Keats—more especially when I am addressing myself to 'the young of both sexes, to whom poetry is, like love, a passion'.

·

Lightning Source UK Ltd.
Milton Keynes UK
UKHW012025290920
370746UK00001B/38